CU00767731

First Published by Nikola Howard in The United Kingdom of
Great Britain and Northern Ireland in 2016.

This edition published in November 2016 by Nikola Howard
ISBN: 1519089449
Imprint: Independently published

Hi there!

Thank you so much for purchasing this eBook, designed to empower you and enable you to create fast and easy menu plans for your low carb way of life.

Enjoy!

TABLE OF CONTENTS

Why Plan?

Converting to a Low Carb lifestyle is a major shift, and when we change our diet to remove what society currently sees as the main keystones of our diets we can be left feeling rather lost. There is such a weight of culture around building meals around the starchy carbohydrate portion, that when this is removed from the equation it can feel as if there is "nothing left" – even if that isn't true.

Nigh on the entirety of civilisation builds its meals and snacks around carbohydrates. Sugar is now ubiquitous and most of Europe and North America uses wheat (the Irish are unusual in choosing potato as their main starch), South America and Africa uses maize and cassava (these became common to Africa after they were introduced by the Portuguese in the 16th Century, supplanting millet, banana and yam as the main starch crops) and Asia generally uses rice. In fact, some countries have even incorporated this into their language; for instance, in Japanese, the work for breakfast is "asa-gohan" (朝ごはん)"Asa" means morning whilst "gohan", which loosely means meal, translates literally as "cooked rice", as all Japanese meals are rice based. Following the logic, lunch is "hiru-gohan" and dinner is "ban-gohan"

Without a plan, radically changing both diet and lifestyle feeling can leave us swimming in uncertainty. From a practical perspective, menu planning can help get over that hump. It can save money and time and creates an easier life. Menu and meal planning can take on any form. At the most basic, simply a written shopping list. it can also be complex, for example, as a calendar chart with recipes, leftovers planning and automatically generated ingredient lists. Or anything in between those two extremes.

As everyone's lifestyle is different, no one way is better than another. One of the things people find hardest about transitioning to a low carb diet, is realising that the nutrient composition of each meal is far more important that what time of day we eat it in. This seems rather radical when we consider how used we are to being marketed all forms of carbohydrates, especially for breakfast.

What needs to change about the food you eat

This way of eating is a large change from the government recommended diet where your daily calorie allowance comprises of the three macronutrients in these ratios: 10-35% protein, 20-30% mostly polyunsaturated fats and 45-60% mostly starchy carbohydrates.

This generally requires eating foods that have been formulated to comply with these ratios. A whole industry of "low fat", "fat free" and processed foods with very high sugar content has become the norm. However, the foods you eat when low carb tend to come packaged by nature in the optimal nutrient balance to satisfy hunger and fulfil the body's needs, and there no need to mess around with them to create tasty and nutritious food.

Scientifically speaking, it is carbohydrate that encourages the secretion of insulin which both drives hunger and converts carbohydrate to body fat, and consumed fat can only turn into body fat when carbohydrate is eaten. This is why a low carbohydrate diet's percentages are balanced more towards protein and fat. When consuming a low carbohydrate diet, where insulin secretion is suppressed, the macronutrients are balanced differently: 20-35% protein, 50-70% monounsaturated and saturated fats and 5-10% mostly vegetable carbohydrates.

You may be asking why is this way of eating so different to a conventional approach? And why so much fat? Because when restricting carbohydrate, your body naturally derives energy from fat, and the presence of dietary fat reassures the body that it's ok for it to burn its stored fat.[1]

---

[1] http://www.lowcarbinthe.uk/blog/why-low-carb-must-be-high-fat

Naturally, if we want to burn fat and obtain a slimmer and healthy body, taking the energy from our fat stores is highly desirable, which the body cannot do when carbohydrate consumption is giving insulin the control over fat storage.

In terms of choices, this boils down to all foods fitting in one of three categories, with foods that provide the balance of nutrients we need are drawn mostly from **optimal** and **sub-optimal** foods. Avoiding the **non-optimal** is simply sensible, they detract from the body, not improve it. [2]

- **Optimal**
    - Nutrient dense protein and saturated/monounsaturated fat containing foods such as meat, fish, fowl, game, eggs, cheese, cream, butter and olive oil as well as leafy vegetables, herbs and spices.
- **Sub-optimal**
    - Nutrient dense low carbohydrate containing foods such as nuts, seeds, onions & garlic, non-root colourful vegetables, legumes and berry fruit.
- **Non-optimal**
    - nutrient sparse foods or very high carbohydrate containing food such as polyunsaturated and hydrogenated fats, alcohol, table sugar, high sugar fruits, honey, flour, bread, potatoes, rice and pasta.

---

[2] Other systems use words that can be used to assign guilt to eating insulin encouraging foods. In my work, I've found that using words such as "banned", "naughty" or "red" means that guilt is usually felt when eating these foods. Letting go of this guilt is a big piece of the mindset shift work that also need to happen to make low carb a way of life, and not "just another diet"

You also need to find the optimum "fuel mix" for your body, as everyone's body reacts differently. Measuring is not required when we eat non processed food as we can rely on our own hunger and satisfaction levels to a much greater extent when sugar is not hitting the addiction centres in our brains.

However, if you do want to quantify, track or measure; try starting with a mix that is calorically 20% protein, 70% fat and 10% carbohydrate. This will start your body running on fat well, and then from there, you can tweak as desired.

Some people feel better with slightly more protein, others more fat – and once your body is fully adjusted to running on fat rather than carbohydrates (this generally takes around 2 months), most people find the best mix is to increase protein and decrease fat, so your body is burning your body fat, not the fat that you consume. For instance, a commonly suggested macronutrient mix for body fat burning is 35% protein, 55% fat and 10% carbohydrate.

If you are the type of person that likes quantifying, the best nutrient calculator I've found is one created by a chap called Martin Ankerl: http://keto-calculator.ankerl.com/ [3]

Once you have your numbers, you can then use these in a variety of online software "nutrient trackers", such as My Fitness Pal, CRON-O-meter and Fat Secret or use good old fashioned pen and paper to keep yourself on track.

---

[3] NB: This is an American tool, so it talks about "net" carbs – UK labelling standards make this distinction irrelevant, our numbers are already minus fibre, and so are automatically "net" http://www.lowcarbinthe.uk/blog/e-mailfaq/#18

Why a calorie is not always a calorie

One of the reasons a low carb way of eating can be seen as controversial is that you do it with no "calorie counting" at all, listening to your body signals and eating to the point of no hunger but no further. There is also no need to make yourself a slave to a complex "food counting" regime as part of your life, unless you are the type of person that likes having the raw data of course!

Conventional wisdom dictates an absolute view that "calories in < calories out = weight loss" - the only way to lose weight is to create an energy deficit by restrict energy intake to below the body's energy output.

It further states that carbohydrate should be the main food choice with a barely sufficient amount of protein and a very limited supplied of calorie rich fat consumed, that having enough will power to ignore hunger is paramount, and suffering is normal and for your greater good.

However, what this doesn't take into account is either our hormonal response to the food we eat or the fact that the body does not use all the food we eat as pure energy.

Simply put, the body does not use all the calories we eat as energy.

- The body uses most of the protein we consume in the constant processes of body maintenance; all of your "soft" body structures are mostly made of protein and no more than 2 weeks old. Even your bones (mostly calcified collagen) are only 10 years old, and so a constant supply of high quality protein is required for this renewal process. The body will only convert protein into carbohydrate that can then feed into the energy cycle in the absence of other energy sources.

- Only a portion of the fats we eat are available for converting into energy, as the body uses cholesterol and other essential fatty acids to create hormones, cell walls and nerve sheathing (myelin).
- Carbohydrate is exclusively used as an energy source, either for burning straight away or putting into either short or long term storage. It has no function in body repair at all.

Also, the lack of calories stimulates the production of the hunger causing hormone ghrelin and carbohydrate containing food stimulate the production of fat-storing hormone insulin, switching off the bodies capabilities to burn its own fat stores.

This means that when eating a carbohydrate focused diet, burning one's own body fat is almost impossible. It's only overnight when digestion has finished and the stomach is empty that fat burning can commence. This means that weight losses seen with low calorie dieting are generally driven by muscle wasting rather than fat reduction. This muscle reduction leads to a reduction in the basal metabolic rate, which results in a rebound fat gain when a more usual level of calorie consumption is resumed, especially if you have the type of body that is pre-disposed to fatten easily[4].

---

[4] http://www.lowcarbinthe.uk/blog/feelings/ and http://www.ourcivilisation.com/fat/chap1.htm

When to Plan

At the simplest level, it is best to plan before you go shopping, around your available budget and also when you are not hungry. The act of planning is an act of self-love and honours your body - you making time to ensure that are taking time to look after it and have the best food for it available enables the needed mindset shifts to take a low carb diet to a successful low carb life. Where the mind goes, the body follows.

Take a break at some point in your day and think about what you like to eat and when, and how food currently fits into your life - you will already have patterns and food that you enjoy. Scribble some notes about what your life allows time-wise to reasonably prepare for each meal, if a meal is regularly eaten "on-the-run" or in a place where you cannot cook food properly or at all, and also write some thoughts around if, when and why you snack and what you snack upon.

Once you have captured these large thoughts, planning week to week will fall out very easily. Having food around that is easy to hand and fits in with your style of eating means that you are far less likely to make non-optimal food choices, especially if you have people in your house who do not eat the same way you do. Planning means that you'll always know you have something in the cupboard to eat, which is reassuring in itself.

How to Plan

Firstly, let's address budget, as there is no getting around the fact that protein is expensive. However, cheaper protein sources are often more flavourful than more expensive ones, and planning to use these helps control budget. Budget can also drive batch cooking, where again the cheaper sources of protein fit in very well.

Note that there is no need to buy outlandish or special foods or gadgets, as this way of eating is very much grounded in using natural ingredients. If someone says to you something along the lines of needing "xyz pre-prepared food or gadget to be a low carb success", ask yourself this simple question: "Can I instantly think of a meal or snack using xyz?" If not, you will simply never use it. When we plan, we honour ourselves and our commitment to a healthy body and de-clutter before "xyz" even has the chance to end up unused in our cupboards.

Secondly, the level of planning that you want do usually depends on the type of person you are. You might be the type of cook that buys similar foods week to week, looks in their fridge and makes something up by riffing off past successes (this is me), or you might like to cook from tried and tested recipes, have lots of variation in what you eat and want to compile detailed weekly or monthly menus. Either way, shopping for it all has to fit in with your life. Most people will plan monthly for canned and frozen foods, fresh vegetables that keep well, seasonings, store-cupboard items and also for general "household" goods such as cleaning products.

With "short-term" perishable foods, aim to plan to shop for them as frequently as fits your cold storage capacity and schedule. For me, a Londoner with a relatively small fridge-freezer, with small supermarkets on my daily commute, this is usually bi-weekly for meat/fish, green vegetables and dairy.

Start with knowing roughly what food you want to obtain and then forming three core lists from these wants, one for "Perishable Foods", one for "Seasonings" and one for "Store Cupboard Ingredients" that will always be in your house.

The foods on the list will need to cover all your meal needs for however long that your plan lasts and you may also want to cover batch cooking planning in these lists if you have a freezer, as batch cooking is a massive time saver in a busy life. Having something in the freezer that can easily be re-heated quickly could be the difference between an optimal healthy meal and an ill-advised take-away pizza if you are too frazzled to cook something.

When eating in a low carbohydrate fashion, hunger is much reduced, so you may well find that you satisfy hunger with 2 meals and a small snack on some days, whereas on others, you will want 3 full meals and a couple of snacks as well! This variation in day to day hunger level is completely normal and there should never be any guilt attached to eating. Remember the first rule, if you are hungry, eat.

Once you have thought about your life and food patterns, you can then get to planning and list building. You can either build the lists manually, or use an automated menu planner/recipe database that generates shopping lists for you. This can also be a time saver – and depending on the application, it can even make the core lists for you, rather than all-in-one lists that you then have to separate out. Several popular recipe websites, like the BBC Good Food site, have an "add to shopping list" button that will gather all the ingredients you need to buy for the recipes you have chosen.

There are also several recipe database and menu planning products on the internet, both desktop based and in cloud, some free and some paid for. As I've not tried any of them, I can't personally recommend at this time. However, if you drop by the LCUK Facebook group, there are many helpful people there:
https://www.facebook.com/groups/lowcarbintheuk/

A special note about breakfast: the challenge deconstructed

For most people breakfast will initially feel like the biggest challenge, as it seems that everything that we are advised to eat for breakfast is off the menu. So, the need to "free your mind" is paramount. In the UK, breakfast is usually carbohydrate based – cereal or toast/bagel/muffin/crumpet (with jam) and orange juice - a meal that sets the body up to ask for more food soon after it is consumed.

Specific "breakfast food" is a very new concept – created by marketers to sell cereals. Before cereal, people simply ate the food they had to hand to break their fast, with only the upper classes having more specific food offerings in the mornings, generally dictated by fashion rather than anything else.

Changing what you eat for breakfast may well be the most radical part of a low carbohydrate way of eating, and planning for that change is vital, so, before we get into our core lists and planning the shopping, let's take a moment to focus on what breakfast now means.

Overnight, when our stomachs empty, our bodies very happily burns stored fats to keep us alive, and so the first meal of the day ideally needs to enable the body to continue this good work. This means that it needs to consist of food that stimulates the fat burning hormone glucagon and suppresses the hunger hormone ghrelin. Food that does not stimulate the fat storing hormone insulin is also key. [5]

---

[5] If you want to know more about the partner actions of glucagon and insulin, along with ghrelin and leptin, go check out this article:
http://www.lowcarbinthe.uk/blog/hormone-balancing/

Insulin secretion, and so fat storage, is stimulated by eating carbohydrate. Ghrelin secretion is suppressed by eating protein, which in turn allows leptin to tell the brain that no more food is required. Glucagon secretion is stimulated by eating protein. Fat has a mild stimulating effect on leptin secretion, but has no effect on the secretion of the other hormones. Fat also stimulates a healthy bowel movement as well as reassuring the body that there are plentiful calories in the now, which means that the body is safe to continue to use up stored body fats.

What does this mean in practice? Eating a satisfying meal of fatty protein is the best way to start the day, as well as to continue it.

As a sidebar, the 1950's marketing slogan "Go to work on an egg" is actually perfect advice. As human food, the egg is virtually perfect, containing the complete spectrum of amino acids, the right amount and quality of fats (and lecithin to aid in emulsifying it) and every mineral and vitamin you are going to need to live thrive and survive, bar Vitamin C. Eggs are a perfectly proportioned, perfect delivery system for nutrition that our bodies love.

There are only so many eggs that a person can eat though, from a mental perspective more than a physical one, which is where "thinking outside the cereal box" comes into play. Breakfast is just another meal, and your body doesn't have any concept of "breakfast food" at all. All food to your body is either energy or building blocks; what we eat at breakfast time is linked to cultural norms, not to body requirement.

Since I chose a low carb way of life in 1999, what I've eaten for week-day breakfast has varied with my ability to cook and prepare one - I eat when I arrive at work, my morning routine is "up and out!" - my breakfast has been through variations of a 100g bag of pecan or macadamia nuts, a chicken salad box from the work canteen, cheese and ham wraps, a creamy protein shake, a tuna and sweetcorn "sandwich-filler" pot, natural full-fat Greek yoghurt with 50g toasted flaked almond and one diced dried apricot, 3 eggs scrambled in the work microwave, a bowl of tuna mayonnaise and a couple of mozzarella balls.

If I'm grabbing breakfast (or any food) on the run somewhere, I usually grab a pack of ham, chicken drumsticks or sliced cheese, or a "sandwich-filler" pot. Life without bread to stop fingers getting messy means that I carry a spoon, a fork and some hand wipes in my handbag, so I don't have to worry about not being able to eat breadless messy snack food.

When I work from home, I usually have either three eggs scrambled with butter and a dash of tomato ketchup, smoked salmon and cream cheese or cream cheese and some pecan nuts (I use the nuts to scoop the cheese direct from the pot).

At the weekend, I either skip breakfast altogether and the first meal I eat will be "lunch" or I have fried eggs and sausages or burgers with maybe some sort of spinach, tomato, shallot and mushroom sauté (whatever vegetables I have in the fridge), a cheese and vegetable omelette or left-overs from the night before.

As you can see, most of these foods are not at all "breakfast" but they all fulfil the criteria of satisfying hunger and encouraging glucagon secretion. There is infinite possibility and once you crack the "breakfast is just another meal" rhythm, most people find that the rest of their plan will very naturally fall into place as "lunch" and "dinner" are far less proscriptive and easier to deal with socially as well as in the kitchen.

Building the core lists

If you are a "look in the fridge/cupboards and make something up" type, then you will have a loose "always have available" set of core food lists. As I am one of this type of people, and to give you an idea of what your lists might look like, here are mine:

My perishables list, I buy from this list when an item is not in my fridge:

- Eggs
- "Meat/fish/chicken"
    - (Mine are usually "steak or burgers/salmon/small whole bird" – Both local food shop is an M&S, so I use their "3 for £10" offers on good quality meat, fish and chicken extensively)
- Double cream
- Full fat Greek yoghurt
- Broccoli
- Hispi cabbage (or savoy, whatever's in season)
- Cauliflower
- Mushrooms
- Peppers
- Smoked salmon
- Cream cheese
- Unsalted butter
- Cheddar cheese
- Pre-sliced cheese to make Cheese Crisps with (http://www.lowcarbinthe.uk/blog/cheese-crisps)

I often vary vegetables in the "green and leafy" section, depending on season (I love flower sprouts with a passion, and I'll then also usually buy a camembert to bake and eat with them), add in a gem or cos lettuce a Chicken Caesar Salad (macadamia nuts makes an excellent crouton substitute) or tuna mayonnaise along with a cucumber and spring onions (firm lettuces make excellent cracker/toast substitutes) and crème fraîche if I am in the mood for a stroganoff. I also buy a few avocados once a month or so and lemons to roast with chicken occasionally.

For me, my perishables list is far more of a general guideline, rather than a strict list. Your core list will almost certainly look rather different.

I also have an "2-day automated" breakfast and lunch list for work, and when I'm there, I usually eat the same meal every day. As of this writing, I buy:

- 4x Mozzarella balls
- 2 packs of Prawns or King Prawns (I used to eat pre-packed chicken, but it started giving me nausea)
- 1 pack salad leaves
- 1 pack full-fat coleslaw

I eat the 2 mozzarella as my breakfast and use a pack of prawns, and half the coleslaw and salad to make lunch with. I also always take a lunch break, as allowing the mind to reset and not think about work for an hour makes for a much more productive afternoon.

My seasonings list encompasses my snack foods, herbs, spices, pastes and anything I often add to food, again, I buy from this list when I've run out of that item:

- Parmesan
- Onions
- Shallots
- Garlic
- Roasted nuts (Almonds, Pecans, Hazelnuts etc)
- Unroasted nuts (Macadamia and Pecans)

- High percentage Chocolate (I personally prefer Hotel Chocolat)
- Turmeric
- Paprika
- Smoked paprika
- Ground Cumin
- Ground Coriander seed
- English Mustard Powder
- Mixed Herbs
- Umami Paste
- Tomato Puree
- Garlic Paste
- Ginger Paste
- Chipotle Chili Paste
- Worcestershire Sauce

This list is very much dictated by day-to-day tastes; Again, I would expect yours to vary from mine.

The store cupboard list is cooking stuffs that are used slowly, such as fats, oils as well as canned goods and non-perishables:

- Olive Oil
- Coconut Oil
- Ghee
- Mayonnaise (full fat, I prefer Hellman's)
- Vinegars (Red Wine/White Wine/Cider/Malt/Balsamic)
- Canned Tuna/Salmon
- Canned Tomato
- Nut Butters
- Ground Almonds for baking
- Unflavoured Whey protein powder

- More rarely used spices and herbs, rock/Himalayan salt, peppercorns

Again, the lists don't even preclude me from buying things I want to try, but they are my essentials - the touchstones that I create with. I have a blackboard on my fridge that I make a note on when I run out of any of my core seasonings and store cupboard items, so that I can easily plan and shop for them online with low stress.

If you are a person that cooks far more to recipes, or wants to regularly batch cook, you will build core lists that are informed by the recipes that you use and like as well the quick foods that you like to have around. Unless you have some software that does the analysis for you, you will need to spend some time building your lists. Once you do this though, you can automate your shopping and give yourself the gift of more time.

Putting it all together

Day-to-day meal planning can be done in several ways, everything from "meal automation" where similar foods are eaten most days (again, this is me) through to wild variation of diet at every meal.

I personally like to think of it in a grid to be filled:

Meal	Monday	Tuesday	Wednesday	Thursday	Friday	Saturday	Sunday
Breakfast							
Lunch							
Dinner							
Snack if desired							
Snack if desired							

You can make any notation that you wish into this type of grid, make notes of the recipe, or add full on nutrient count, with a total row at the bottom of the table if you are into collecting the data. You can slot things into the grid easily, use a notebook to write in or make something fancy with some spreadsheet software that will add everything up for you. This is very much around how it will fit your life

This style of plan is especially helpful where you are quantifying what you eat as well as simply planning it, especially if you are working to recipes where you already know the macronutrient content.

To give you an example, my "pre-filled" grid would look like this at the start of most weeks, and fits my life in this manner:

Meal	Monday	Tuesday	Wednesday	Thursday	Friday	Saturday	Sunday
Breakfast	2x Mozzarella	2x Mozzarella	3x Scrambled Eggs	3x Scrambled eggs	2x Mozzarella	N/A	N/A
Lunch	Prawn Salad	Prawn Salad	??	??	Prawn Salad	??	??
Dinner	??	??	??	??	??	??	??
Snack if desired	~100g Roasted nuts	~100g Roasted nuts	Few spoonfuls of Nut butter	Few spoonfuls of Nut butter	~100g Roasted nuts	~100g Roasted nuts	Few spoonfuls of Nut butter
Snack if desired	~30g of high% chocolate	~30g of high% chocolate	~30g of high% chocolate	~30g of high% chocolate	~30g of high% chocolate	~30g of high% chocolate	~30g of high% chocolate

As I'm a "make it up" type cook, I never have set meals for dinner or on weekends, as this is when I looking in the fridge to see what I fancy. Some days I snack, others I don't, if I'm hungry, I eat! I generally only eat two meals at the weekend, tend to have at least one evening where I don't eat dinner at all, usually eat out at least once a week with friends, and, I "automate" at work weekday breakfast and lunch.

My question marks are filled with a rotation of variations on:

- Steak, broccoli, cabbage or cauliflower with cream mushroom & peppercorn sauce
- Fried salmon, cooked in ghee & broccoli with olive oil or mayonnaise dressing
- Burger & cabbage or broccoli, cheese sauce
- Lemon and garlic roast chicken and vegetables with the juices
- Beef stroganoff (using cabbage ribbons as the "noodle" sub)

- Bolognaise ragu with courgetti or cabbage ribbons
- Leftovers from any of the above!
- Tuna mayonnaise
- Salmon & cream cheese
- Chicken livers and salad, olive oil & balsamic dressing

When eating out I pick a main that comes with vegetables or actively ask to swap a potato or rice side for a salad or whatever green vegetables they offer. Restaurants are usually very accommodating, as the essence of good service is giving the customer what they want. Since 1999, in all the meals I've eaten out with friends, it's been rare that I've had trouble finding anything to eat at all.

Eating take-away works in a similar vein, and tends to be even easier - Naturally, take away pizza and chips are off the menu, but in terms of Indian, Chinese, or most other types of take away, order the "meat" dish of your favourite take away meal and buy a vegetable side rather than the usual rice.

How to deal with exceptions

Unfortunately, there are always times when the only choice is a non-optimal one or we make a choice that is not to our body's benefit - a non-optimal food crosses your path (my weakness is chips) and you chose to either eat it or not to make an optimal choice instead of a non-optimal one (in my case, that's a side of chips rather than a side of salad.)

If you know that a difficult situation is coming, you might even choose to plan to take a "nutritional vacation", but if you do make this choice, then deal with that choice as an adult, from a strong mindful position and not as a victim; own your choice, eat with no guilt, take a drink of water and simply move on to your next healthy mouthful.

A non-optimal food choice is never an excuse to wreck your life, it's just food after all. Commit to the decision to make many more optimal choices than non-optimal ones, and your mind and body will work very happily together.

There are also views that an occasional wobble is a good thing - the body is evolved to deal with "the unusual" (this mechanism is called "hormesis") and by occasional throwing something bizarre into the mix, it helps your body to hone its response and stay optimal - it also helps you to understand the signals your body used to tell you "I didn't like that!" or "More of that stuff please!" A blip is just that, a blip - learn all you can from it and move on.

Wrapping up

Thank you so much for reading, and I hope that this eBook has empowered you to create fast and easy menu plans for your low carb way of life

Drop me an e-mail at eBooks@lowcarbinthe.uk if you want to talk about anything covered in this eBook, and if you do however feel inspired, and ready to go for planning your low carb life, I would suggest your next steps are:

- Investigating the many articles on my website: http://www.lowcarbinthe.uk as further reading,
- Joining the Facebook group for this book: https://www.facebook.com/groups/190755661359100/
    - Or the general LCUK Facebook group https://www.facebook.com/groups/lowcarbintheuk/
- Watching my masterclass webinars: http://www.lowcarbinthe.uk/digital/
- Take my: "The hunger free way to a slimmer you: Ten easy shifts to a low carb way of life eCourse
- And using my 1:1 personal coaching offerings to help you: http://www.lowcarbinthe.uk/work-with-me/

Thank you for reading!

Printed in Great Britain
by Amazon